Draw near to God, and he will draw near to you.

JAMES 4:8

THE NEAR JOURNAL

An uncomplicated yet empowering way for you to draw near to God, simplify your life, and be happier.

FOUNDATIONS

Welcome to the *Near Journal*, a straightforward and honest way to develop and strengthen lifelong Christian habits that will change your life and bring you closer to God.

I've been a Christian for a long time, and I always felt I was missing something. I felt there were an overwhelming amount of things I needed to do. Unfortunately, it was very difficult for me to do even the easiest things, like reading scripture and praying, on a consistent basis.

It all seemed so confusing and overwhelming. Many of my friends felt the same way. Even if we did go to church, it sometimes just made us feel more frustrated at ourselves since we weren't doing what we knew we should be doing.

So I started looking for a way to solve my problem. Surely there was some sort of notebook or devotional that could help me stay organized spiritually, and help keep me on track—with both the easy and more difficult pieces of the Christian walk. No matter how hard I looked, I couldn't find anything that would help.

That's when I decided to create the *Near Journal* to solve my own problem. The elements contained within this journal have helped me tremendously in my own personal walk with God. Now I'm releasing it to the public, so that you can experience the same benefits that I have received.

Jacob Vandenbark

DESIGNED AND PRINTED IN THE UNITED STATES OF AMERICA.
SECOND EDITION.

ISBN 978-0-578-65167-5

CONTACT US FOR INFORMATION ABOUT DISTRIBUTION AND SPECIAL DISCOUNTS AVAILABLE FOR BULK PURCHASES.

DRAW NEAR CO.
WWW.DRAWNEAR.CO
HELLO@DRAWNEAR.CO

TABLE OF CONTENTS

FIVE ANCHORS OF SUCCESS

The *Near Journal* blends together five key components to help facilitate your spiritual growth and give you direction and focus. These ingredients form a simple daily framework that fit into what you want to do: whether it is reading the Bible yourself or complementing a normal bible study or devotional book.

1. *Room to Write*

Each day there is a large chunk of space left empty for your thoughts and ideas. Feel free to write about what's on your mind, things you found interesting in what you read, or if you are feeling stuck you can read through the writing prompts provided on page 16 to help engage your mind and give you ideas to write about.

2. *Personal Growth and Accountability*

The actions you take turn into the habits you create. The Bible tells us that we, as believers, will be known by our fruit. The *Near Journal* helps you choose an area of focus and gives you prompts each day to help you plan for the future, think about current progress, and take action in areas that matter. It's devotion paired with action!

"Do not merely listen to the Word and so deceive yourselves. Do what it says."

JAMES 1:22

3. *Cultivating Thankfulness*

Gratitude is extremely important. It keeps us in a positive frame of mind, and regardless of our scenario it improves the satisfaction that we have with our life. A study by UC Davis psychologist Robert Emmons, the world's leading scientific expert on gratitude, proved that keeping a gratitude journal can significantly improve our well-being and happiness. Each day, there is space provided for you to jot down what you are grateful for.

"Give thanks in all circumstances;
for this is God's will for you..."
1 THESSALONIANS 5:18

4. *Power of Prayer*

Prayer is a gift that connects us directly with God. God hears our prayers and answers them. The *Near Journal* provides a designated place for you to track the things you are praying about and the prayers that God has answered in your life. We recommend dividing the prayer section into two components: "Yourself" and "Others." This gives you room to track your personal and internal prayers for yourself and also room to track your prayers for your family, friends, and the world.

5. *Memorization of Scripture*

Knowing God's word is a cornerstone of the Christian faith. Each day there are simple prompts that help you memorize different Bible verses. A wide variety of memorization techniques are incorporated to assist with memorization. Feel free to adjust the prompts to fit your personal needs and learning styles.

PERSONAL GROWTH

There is a great quote by Henry Drummond, a Scottist writer and evangelist from the 1800s, that I love:

"If a man does not exercise his arm he develops no biceps muscle; and if a man does not exercise his soul, he acquires no muscle in his soul, no strength of character, no vigor of moral fiber, nor beauty of Spiritual growth."

The strength of your relationship with God and the pace of your spiritual growth is often tied closely to your level of spiritual effort, because God calls us to continually take up our crosses daily and follow Him—and that means looking more and more like Him every day.

Self-improvement is a difficult thing (as proven by the fact there is an entire section for it at the bookstore), and it is made more difficult by lack of focus. It is tough to improve multiple things at once. This is the main reason why most New Year's Resolutions fail. People try to go to the gym, read more books, eat healthier, and keep their house clean all at the same time. They don't focus on nailing down the most important thing first.

The only thing working on multiple items at once accomplishes, is it reduces the effort you can apply to the one thing that would make the most impact in your life. When you have two goals, you cannot give your best effort to the most important one.

For the next 90 days, you are going to focus on **one thing** that you want to improve. Each day there will be prompts to remind you of your area of focus and help keep you on track.

Are you ready?

Area of Focus

What big area of your life do you want to improve in the next 90 days? What benefits would you see if you were to improve in this area? Try to choose something specific and personally rewarding. Bonus points if improving in this area will make it easier for you to improve in other areas: for example if you work on being more peaceful, that will make it easier to quit cussing.

Support Pillars

What specific things do you need to do in order to improve in your area of focus over the next 90 days?

1. . . . .

. . . .

2. . . . .

. . . .

3. . . . .

. . . .

The Why

What makes you want to improve in this area? How will your life, your walk with God, and your mental state improve if you hit your goal?

. . . .

. . . .

. . . .

. . . .

Commit

A big part of progress is being serious about making progress. You will experience some trials, you might slip up, and it won't be easy. Are you ready to do what it takes to make some progress? If so sign your name below and consider sharing your goal with someone that you can trust (and someone you can talk to in 90 days from now about how well you've done).

. . . .

[SIGN HERE]

MEMORIZE

Memorizing scripture is important: the Bible tells us to "store up His word in our hearts, that we might not sin against God."

Being able to easily recall specific bible verses helps us fight temptation (just like Jesus did in the wilderness when being tempted by Satan). It also helps us quickly offer words of encouragement and truth to people that we care about, and it helps us to know what God wants for us on a deeper level.

When we have memorized scripture, it gets into our soul and we can use it to fellowship with God and remember his promises more readily. Colossians 3:16 tells us to "let the word of Christ dwell in us richly" and memorization is an excellent way to do that.

How It Works

Over the next 90 days, you'll memorize nine different bible verses which you can use to help you in your daily walk with God. Each verse follows a nine day path of different memorization prompts that have been crafted to speed up and solidify the memorization process.

Tip: Choose verses that relate to the area of focus you just chose!

In the space below, spend some time choosing the verses that you want to memorize. If you are unsure where to start, read through the recommended verses on the next page. I also recommend downloading a Bible app and searching for a keyword you are interested in (love, peace, etc)—that's a simple way to find good verses.

Verse Selection

EXAMPLE: Joshua 1:8 . . . .

1. . . . .
2. . . . .
3. . . . .
4. . . . .
5. . . . .
6. . . . .
7. . . . .
8. . . . .
9. . . . .

RECOMMENDED MEMORIZATION VERSES

If you don't know where to start, here is an excellent list of verses that we recommend memorizing. Take a look at them and see which ones you think would benefit you based on what you are dealing with right now.

Joshua 1:8

Psalms 145:18-19

Psalms 27:1

Psalms 56:3-4

Psalms 119:11

Proverbs 3:5-6

Matthew 6:33

Matthew 6:19-21

Matthew 22:37-39

John 3:16

John 6:40

John 8:31-32

John 14:6

Romans 12:1-2

Romans 8:38-39

Romans 6:23

Romans 3:23

1 Corinthians 13:4-7

1 Corinthians 10:13

2 Corinthians 12:9

Galatians 2:20

Galatians 5:1

Galatians 5:22-23

Ephesians 2:4-5

Philippians 4:19

Philippians 4:6-7

Hebrews 4:16

Hebrews 12:1-2

James 1:12

James 1:27

1 John 3:18

THOUGHTS AND REFLECTION PROMPTS

Each day, you have a designated space to write your thoughts and reflections about the scripture that you read or anything else on your mind. We all go through writer's block occasionally (or maybe you read a particularly boring bit of Leviticus), so these prompts are provided to get your brain going. Choose one and think about the implications to help you kickstart your journaling.

If every Christian acted just like you, what would the world look like?

THINK ABOUT GOD'S FORGIVENESS. HE CAN FORGIVE ANYTHING—ARE YOU FORGIVING YOURSELF?

Have you thought about doing something for God recently, but you didn't do it? What was it, and why didn't you follow through?

God is our stronghold and fortress. How has God protected you?

Imagine talking to King Solomon, the wisest man in the world. What would you ask for his advice on, and how do you think he'd respond?

What is something that you know you should do, but haven't done yet? How would you feel if you did it, and how would you feel if you never do it?

What injustice in the world makes you really frustrated or angry? How can you show the love of Christ in that situation and take some small action this week to help fix it?

Humble yourself. God made you, and you could never exist without him. In the scope of eternity you are so small, yet God takes an interest in you.

THINK ABOUT THE FACT THAT YOUR SIN ABSOLUTELY SEPARATES YOU FROM GOD, FORFEITS YOUR PLACE IN PARADISE, AND REJECTS HIS ETERNAL LOVE. DESPITE YOUR ACTIONS, GOD FORGIVES YOU.

When have you ever heard a story where the hero dies for the villain? That's what God did, and it is amazing.

If we draw near to God, he will draw near to us. What is the next step you need to take to draw even closer to God?

Think how even small changes in your past could have totally altered your life. The changes you make every day have the same potential—how will you use this power?

There is someone in the world who is worse off than you are, regardless of your current situation. In what ways are you blessed, even in the middle of a tough time?

Think about God's seemingly opposing qualities: His love and strength, righteous anger and tenderness, truth and forgiveness. How does this make you feel, and how can you be more like God in this area?

Imagine being a disciple of Jesus and living a normal day with him. No miracles and no crowds—just a day with Jesus walking along the road, resting, and eating. How would he act?

What are you worrying about? Why are you still holding on to that worry? What would it take for you to release it to God?

Imagine you are looking at your life, actions, habits, and decisions from your best friend's eyes. What would you tell yourself?

DRAW NEAR TO GOD,
AND HE WILL DRAW NEAR TO YOU.
JAMES 4:8

TODAY mm/dd/yy, I READ Philippians 1

YOU CAN WRITE ABOUT WHAT YOU READ, WHAT'S ON YOUR MIND, OR JUST WHAT IS GOING ON IN YOUR LIFE.

WRITE: YOUR THOUGHTS & REFLECTIONS

It is relieving that God has begun a good work in me, and HE will carry it on until the day of completion. This takes a lot of stress off me, because it isn't all about me. I need to remember this.

Paul prays that love would increase, and he specifically mentions it increasing in knowledge and depth of insight. This is interesting, because I think these day, most people would just pray that people would have love, and not tie it to anything.

Paul has so much hope. Whether he is in jail, or people are preaching Christ with false motives, or even if he dies - he is still hopeful. "For me, to live is Christ and to die is gain." That is powerful, especially since I often feel hopeless. Paul clearly didn't get his hope from his circumstances - it came from Christ.

I need to be more hopeful. Hope helps me persevere in the middle of tough times. God, help me to hope in you, and you alone.

FOCUS: ON YOUR PROGRESS AND GOALS

What is one specific action you can take in the next week to move closer to your goal?

This week, I will set an alarm on my phone in the morning as a reminder to read the Bible, and I won't drink a cup of coffee until I've read at least one chapter of the Bible.

THANKS: BLESSINGS & GRATITUDE

- The ability to enjoy good music
- The love I have for my family, and the joy they bring me
- my car, that gets me to and from work

PRAY: REQUESTS & RESULTS FOR YOURSELF & OTHERS

MYSELF	OTHERS
• Peace when things go wrong at work	• my mom's neck to heal
• Self-control and not spending so much time on my phone.	• That our country would experience the peace and love of Christ.
• That I would forgive myself	• Thank you for providing for my brother
• Thank you for answering my prayer and giving me perseverance	

USE THIS SPACE TO TRACK NOT ONLY WHAT YOU ARE PRAYING FOR, BUT PRAYERS THAT GOD HAS ANSWERED FOR YOU. I RECOMMEND DIVIDING THE SPACE UP INTO TWO SECTIONS: "MYSELF" AND "OTHERS."

MEMORIZE: VERSE 1

Flip to page 14, and look at verse 1. Read the verse a few times and think about why this verse is important to you. Write down how having this verse memorized will help you in your walk with God.

Having Joshua 1:8 memorized will help me remember to meditate on the word more continually, and I will grow when I memorize and dwell on God's word. It will give me a reason to keep memorizing.

TODAY ____ / ____ / ____ , I READ ____________________

WRITE: YOUR THOUGHTS & REFLECTIONS

FOCUS: ON YOUR PROGRESS AND GOALS

What is one specific action you can take in the next week to move closer to your goal?

THANKS: BLESSINGS & GRATITUDE

-
-
-

PRAY: REQUESTS & RESULTS FOR YOURSELF & OTHERS

MEMORIZE: VERSE 1

Flip to page 14, and look at verse 1. Read the verse a few times and think about why this verse is important to you. Write down how having this verse memorized will help you in your walk with God.

TODAY ..../..../...., I READ ....

WRITE: YOUR THOUGHTS & REFLECTIONS

FOCUS: ON YOUR PROGRESS AND GOALS

What challenge or temptation can you see yourself possibly having in the next couple of days related to your Area of Focus? How will you respond to this challenge if it arises?

HANKS: BLESSINGS & GRATITUDE

PRAY: REQUESTS & RESULTS FOR YOURSELF & OTHERS

MEMORIZE: VERSE 1

Read the verse out loud five times and silently five times. Be sure to read the book name and verse number, as this is important to memorize also. Write the verse once.

TODAY . . . / . . . / . . . , I READ . . . .

WRITE: YOUR THOUGHTS & REFLECTIONS

FOCUS: ON YOUR PROGRESS AND GOALS

Write a simple prayer to God, asking him to help you improve something specific related to your Area of Focus.

THANKS: BLESSINGS & GRATITUDE

-
-
-

PRAY: REQUESTS & RESULTS FOR YOURSELF & OTHERS

MEMORIZE: VERSE 1

Read the verse five times out loud. Write the verse five times. There are blank pages in the back of this journal that you can use.

TODAY ..../..../...., I READ ....

WRITE: YOUR THOUGHTS & REFLECTIONS

FOCUS: ON YOUR PROGRESS AND GOALS

Look up a bible verse that relates to your area of focus and write it below. Consider if this brings any new insight into your area of focus.

THANKS: BLESSINGS & GRATITUDE

- ...
- ...
- ...

PRAY: REQUESTS & RESULTS FOR YOURSELF & OTHERS

MEMORIZE: VERSE 1

Read the verse out loud once. Then write the verse five times and say the verse to yourself while you are writing.

TODAY ..../..../...., I READ ....

WRITE: YOUR THOUGHTS & REFLECTIONS

FOCUS: ON YOUR PROGRESS AND GOALS

Reflect on the positive progress you've made over the last few days, and write any thoughts about the success you've had so far.

THANKS: BLESSINGS & GRATITUDE

PRAY: REQUESTS & RESULTS FOR YOURSELF & OTHERS

MEMORIZE: VERSE 1

Read the verse out loud once. Write the verse once. Now, without looking try to say the verse. Note where you have trouble and try to say the verse from memory five more times. Review the verse between each attempt to ensure you are correct.

TODAY ..../..../...., I READ ....

WRITE: YOUR THOUGHTS & REFLECTIONS

FOCUS: ON YOUR PROGRESS AND GOALS

Reflect on any difficulties you've had over the last few days, and write any thoughts about what was difficult.

THANKS: BLESSINGS & GRATITUDE

-
-
-

PRAY: REQUESTS & RESULTS FOR YOURSELF & OTHERS

MEMORIZE: VERSE 1

Without reading or looking at the verse, try to say it from memory. After your attempt, look at the verse and see how close you were. Try to repeat the verse five more times, both out loud and silently, looking at the verse as needed.

TODAY ..../..../...., I READ ....

WRITE: YOUR THOUGHTS & REFLECTIONS

FOCUS: ON YOUR PROGRESS AND GOALS

What is one mini action you can take in the next 24 hours that will move you a bit closer to your goal?

THANKS: BLESSINGS & GRATITUDE

•

•

•

PRAY: REQUESTS & RESULTS FOR YOURSELF & OTHERS

MEMORIZE: VERSE 1

Without reading or looking at the verse, try to write it from memory. After your attempt, look at the verse and see how close you were. Try to write the verse five times, and refer back to the verse after each attempt to see how well you did.

TODAY ...../...../....., I READ ....

WRITE: YOUR THOUGHTS & REFLECTIONS

FOCUS: ON YOUR PROGRESS AND GOALS

Reread what you wrote for your Area of Focus and Support Pillars. Are you on the right track to hit your goals? Reaffirm your commitment to stay focused on improving this area of your life.

THANKS: BLESSINGS & GRATITUDE

PRAY: REQUESTS & RESULTS FOR YOURSELF & OTHERS

MEMORIZE: VERSE 1

Say the verse and then write the verse from memory. Then, practice memorizing the verse using whichever technique you've liked the most—do it five times.

TODAY . . . / . . . / . . . , I READ . . . .

WRITE: YOUR THOUGHTS & REFLECTIONS

FOCUS: ON YOUR PROGRESS AND GOALS

Did you complete the action and mini action you set for yourself over the last 8 days? If so, how did it feel to make some progress? If not, what barriers prevented you from completing the actions you set for yourself?.

THANKS: BLESSINGS & GRATITUDE

-
-
-

PRAY: REQUESTS & RESULTS FOR YOURSELF & OTHERS

MEMORIZE: VERSE 1

Say the verse from memory. Pray the verse to God and ask him to help you apply what you have memorized and use it in your life. Write down an example of how knowing this verse from memory could be useful to you.

TODAY ..../..../...., I READ ....

WRITE: YOUR THOUGHTS & REFLECTIONS

FOCUS: ON YOUR PROGRESS AND GOALS

What is one specific action you can take in the next week to move closer to your goal?

THANKS: BLESSINGS & GRATITUDE

-
-
-

PRAY: REQUESTS & RESULTS FOR YOURSELF & OTHERS

MEMORIZE: VERSE 2

Flip to page 14, and look at verse 2. Read the verse a few times and think about why this verse is important to you. Write down how having this verse memorized will help you in your walk with God.

TODAY . . . / . . . / . . . , I READ . . . .

WRITE: YOUR THOUGHTS & REFLECTIONS

FOCUS: ON YOUR PROGRESS AND GOALS

What challenge or temptation can you see yourself possibly having in the next couple of days related to your Area of Focus? How will you respond to this challenge if it arises?

HANKS: BLESSINGS & GRATITUDE

RAY: REQUESTS & RESULTS FOR YOURSELF & OTHERS

MEMORIZE: VERSE 2

Read the verse out loud five times and silently five times. Be sure to read the book name and verse number, as this is important to memorize also. Write the verse once.

TODAY ..../..../...., I READ ....

WRITE: YOUR THOUGHTS & REFLECTIONS

FOCUS: ON YOUR PROGRESS AND GOALS

Write a simple prayer to God, asking him to help you improve something specific related to your Area of Focus.

THANKS: BLESSINGS & GRATITUDE

-
-
-

PRAY: REQUESTS & RESULTS FOR YOURSELF & OTHERS

MEMORIZE: VERSE 2

Read the verse five times out loud. Write the verse five times. There are blank pages in the back of this journal that you can use.

TODAY ..../..../...., I READ ....

WRITE: YOUR THOUGHTS & REFLECTIONS

FOCUS: ON YOUR PROGRESS AND GOALS

Look up a bible verse that relates to your area of focus and write it below. Consider if this brings any new insight into your area of focus.

THANKS: BLESSINGS & GRATITUDE

-
-
-

PRAY: REQUESTS & RESULTS FOR YOURSELF & OTHERS

MEMORIZE: VERSE 2

Read the verse out loud once. Then write the verse five times and say the verse to yourself while you are writing.

TODAY ..../..../...., I READ ....

WRITE: YOUR THOUGHTS & REFLECTIONS

FOCUS: ON YOUR PROGRESS AND GOALS

Reflect on the positive progress you've made over the last few days, and write any thoughts about the success you've had so far.

HANKS: BLESSINGS & GRATITUDE

RAY: REQUESTS & RESULTS FOR YOURSELF & OTHERS

MEMORIZE: VERSE 2

Read the verse out loud once. Write the verse once. Now, without looking try to say the verse. Note where you have trouble and try to say the verse from memory five more times. Review the verse between each attempt to ensure you are correct.

TODAY . . . / . . . / . . . , I READ . . . .

WRITE: YOUR THOUGHTS & REFLECTIONS

FOCUS: ON YOUR PROGRESS AND GOALS

Reflect on any difficulties you've had over the last few days, and write any thoughts about what was difficult.

THANKS: BLESSINGS & GRATITUDE

- ...
- ...
- ...

PRAY: REQUESTS & RESULTS FOR YOURSELF & OTHERS

MEMORIZE: VERSE 2

Without reading or looking at the verse, try to say it from memory. After your attempt, look at the verse and see how close you were. Try to repeat the verse five more times, both out loud and silently, looking at the verse as needed.

TODAY ___ / ___ / ___, I READ ______________________

WRITE: YOUR THOUGHTS & REFLECTIONS

FOCUS: ON YOUR PROGRESS AND GOALS

What is one mini action you can take in the next 24 hours that will move you a bit closer to your goal?

THANKS: BLESSINGS & GRATITUDE

-
-
-

PRAY: REQUESTS & RESULTS FOR YOURSELF & OTHERS

MEMORIZE: VERSE 2

Without reading or looking at the verse, try to write it from memory. After your attempt, look at the verse and see how close you were. Try to write the verse five times, and refer back to the verse after each attempt to see how well you did.

TODAY ..../..../...., I READ ....

WRITE: YOUR THOUGHTS & REFLECTIONS

FOCUS: ON YOUR PROGRESS AND GOALS

Reread what you wrote for your Area of Focus and Support Pillars. Are you on the right track to hit your goals? Reaffirm your commitment to stay focused on improving this area of your life.

'HANKS: BLESSINGS & GRATITUDE

ᴾRAY: REQUESTS & RESULTS FOR YOURSELF & OTHERS

MEMORIZE: VERSE 2

Say the verse and then write the verse from memory. Then, practice memorizing the verse using whichever technique you've liked the most—do it five times.

TODAY . . . / . . . / . . . , I READ . . . .

WRITE: YOUR THOUGHTS & REFLECTIONS

FOCUS: ON YOUR PROGRESS AND GOALS

Did you complete the action and mini action you set for yourself over the last 8 days? If so, how did it feel to make some progress? If not, what barriers prevented you from completing the actions you set for yourself?.

THANKS: BLESSINGS & GRATITUDE

- ....
- ....
- ....

PRAY: REQUESTS & RESULTS FOR YOURSELF & OTHERS

MEMORIZE: VERSE 2

Say the verse from memory. Pray the verse to God and ask him to help you apply what you have memorized and use it in your life. Write down an example of how knowing this verse from memory could be useful to you.

TODAY ..../..../...., I READ ....

WRITE: YOUR THOUGHTS & REFLECTIONS

FOCUS: ON YOUR PROGRESS AND GOALS

What is one specific action you can take in the next week to move closer to your goal?

THANKS: BLESSINGS & GRATITUDE

-
-
-

PRAY: REQUESTS & RESULTS FOR YOURSELF & OTHERS

MEMORIZE: VERSE 3

Flip to page 14, and look at verse 3. Read the verse a few times and think about why this verse is important to you. Write down how having this verse memorized will help you in your walk with God.

TODAY ..../..../...., I READ ....

WRITE: YOUR THOUGHTS & REFLECTIONS

FOCUS: ON YOUR PROGRESS AND GOALS

What challenge or temptation can you see yourself possibly having in the next couple of days related to your Area of Focus? How will you respond to this challenge if it arises?

HANKS: BLESSINGS & GRATITUDE

PRAY: REQUESTS & RESULTS FOR YOURSELF & OTHERS

MEMORIZE: VERSE 3

Read the verse out loud five times and silently five times. Be sure to read the book name and verse number, as this is important to memorize also. Write the verse once.

TODAY ..../..../...., I READ ....

WRITE: YOUR THOUGHTS & REFLECTIONS

FOCUS: ON YOUR PROGRESS AND GOALS

Write a simple prayer to God, asking him to help you improve something specific related to your Area of Focus.

THANKS: BLESSINGS & GRATITUDE

-
-
-

PRAY: REQUESTS & RESULTS FOR YOURSELF & OTHERS

MEMORIZE: VERSE 3

Read the verse five times out loud. Write the verse five times. There are blank pages in the back of this journal that you can use.

TODAY ..../..../...., I READ ....

WRITE: YOUR THOUGHTS & REFLECTIONS

FOCUS: ON YOUR PROGRESS AND GOALS

Look up a bible verse that relates to your area of focus and write it below. Consider if this brings any new insight into your area of focus.

THANKS: BLESSINGS & GRATITUDE

-
-
-

PRAY: REQUESTS & RESULTS FOR YOURSELF & OTHERS

MEMORIZE: VERSE 3

Read the verse out loud once. Then write the verse five times and say the verse to yourself while you are writing.

TODAY ___/___/___, I READ ______________________________

WRITE: YOUR THOUGHTS & REFLECTIONS

FOCUS: ON YOUR PROGRESS AND GOALS

Reflect on the positive progress you've made over the last few days, and write any thoughts about the success you've had so far.

HANKS: BLESSINGS & GRATITUDE

RAY: REQUESTS & RESULTS FOR YOURSELF & OTHERS

MEMORIZE: VERSE 3

Read the verse out loud once. Write the verse once. Now, without looking try to say the verse. Note where you have trouble and try to say the verse from memory five more times. Review the verse between each attempt to ensure you are correct.

TODAY . . . / . . . / . . . , I READ . . . .

WRITE: YOUR THOUGHTS & REFLECTIONS

FOCUS: ON YOUR PROGRESS AND GOALS

Reflect on any difficulties you've had over the last few days, and write any thoughts about what was difficult.

THANKS: BLESSINGS & GRATITUDE

-
-
-

PRAY: REQUESTS & RESULTS FOR YOURSELF & OTHERS

MEMORIZE: VERSE 3

Without reading or looking at the verse, try to say it from memory. After your attempt, look at the verse and see how close you were. Try to repeat the verse five more times, both out loud and silently, looking at the verse as needed.

TODAY . . . / . . . / . . . , I READ . . . .

WRITE: YOUR THOUGHTS & REFLECTIONS

FOCUS: ON YOUR PROGRESS AND GOALS

What is one mini action you can take in the next 24 hours that will move you a bit closer to your goal?

THANKS: BLESSINGS & GRATITUDE

-
-
-

PRAY: REQUESTS & RESULTS FOR YOURSELF & OTHERS

MEMORIZE: VERSE 3

Without reading or looking at the verse, try to write it from memory. After your attempt, look at the verse and see how close you were. Try to write the verse five times, and refer back to the verse after each attempt to see how well you did.

TODAY . . . / . . . / . . . , I READ . . . .

WRITE: YOUR THOUGHTS & REFLECTIONS

FOCUS: ON YOUR PROGRESS AND GOALS

Reread what you wrote for your Area of Focus and Support Pillars. Are you on the right track to hit your goals? Reaffirm your commitment to stay focused on improving this area of your life.

HANKS: BLESSINGS & GRATITUDE

RAY: REQUESTS & RESULTS FOR YOURSELF & OTHERS

MEMORIZE: VERSE 3

Say the verse and then write the verse from memory. Then, practice memorizing the verse using whichever technique you've liked the most—do it five times.

TODAY . . . / . . . / . . . , I READ . . . .

WRITE: YOUR THOUGHTS & REFLECTIONS

FOCUS: ON YOUR PROGRESS AND GOALS

Did you complete the action and mini action you set for yourself over the last 8 days? If so, how did it feel to make some progress? If not, what barriers prevented you from completing the actions you set for yourself?.

THANKS: BLESSINGS & GRATITUDE

-
-
-

PRAY: REQUESTS & RESULTS FOR YOURSELF & OTHERS

MEMORIZE: VERSE 3

Say the verse from memory. Pray the verse to God and ask him to help you apply what you have memorized and use it in your life. Write down an example of how knowing this verse from memory could be useful to you.

TODAY . . . / . . . / . . . , I READ . . . .

WRITE: YOUR THOUGHTS & REFLECTIONS

FOCUS: ON YOUR PROGRESS AND GOALS

What is one specific action you can take in the next week to move closer to your goal?

THANKS: BLESSINGS & GRATITUDE

-
-
-

PRAY: REQUESTS & RESULTS FOR YOURSELF & OTHERS

MEMORIZE: VERSE 4

Flip to page 14, and look at verse 4. Read the verse a few times and think about why this verse is important to you. Write down how having this verse memorized will help you in your walk with God.

TODAY ..../..../...., I READ ....

WRITE: YOUR THOUGHTS & REFLECTIONS

FOCUS: ON YOUR PROGRESS AND GOALS

What challenge or temptation can you see yourself possibly having in the next couple of days related to your Area of Focus? How will you respond to this challenge if it arises?

HANKS: BLESSINGS & GRATITUDE

RAY: REQUESTS & RESULTS FOR YOURSELF & OTHERS

MEMORIZE: VERSE 4

Read the verse out loud five times and silently five times. Be sure to read the book name and verse number, as this is important to memorize also. Write the verse once.

TODAY ..../..../....., I READ ....

WRITE: YOUR THOUGHTS & REFLECTIONS

FOCUS: ON YOUR PROGRESS AND GOALS

Write a simple prayer to God, asking him to help you improve something specific related to your Area of Focus.

THANKS: BLESSINGS & GRATITUDE

- . . . .
- . . . .
- . . . .

PRAY: REQUESTS & RESULTS FOR YOURSELF & OTHERS

MEMORIZE: VERSE 4

Read the verse five times out loud. Write the verse five times. There are blank pages in the back of this journal that you can use.

TODAY . . . / . . . / . . . , I READ . . . .

WRITE: YOUR THOUGHTS & REFLECTIONS

FOCUS: ON YOUR PROGRESS AND GOALS

Look up a bible verse that relates to your area of focus and write it below. Consider if this brings any new insight into your area of focus.

THANKS: BLESSINGS & GRATITUDE

-
-
-

PRAY: REQUESTS & RESULTS FOR YOURSELF & OTHERS

MEMORIZE: VERSE 4

Read the verse out loud once. Then write the verse five times and say the verse to yourself while you are writing.

TODAY ___/___/___, I READ ______________________

WRITE: YOUR THOUGHTS & REFLECTIONS

FOCUS: ON YOUR PROGRESS AND GOALS

Reflect on the positive progress you've made over the last few days, and write any thoughts about the success you've had so far.

HANKS: BLESSINGS & GRATITUDE

RAY: REQUESTS & RESULTS FOR YOURSELF & OTHERS

MEMORIZE: VERSE 4

Read the verse out loud once. Write the verse once. Now, without looking try to say the verse. Note where you have trouble and try to say the verse from memory five more times. Review the verse between each attempt to ensure you are correct.

TODAY ... / ... / ... , I READ ...

WRITE: YOUR THOUGHTS & REFLECTIONS

FOCUS: ON YOUR PROGRESS AND GOALS

Reflect on any difficulties you've had over the last few days, and write any thoughts about what was difficult.

THANKS: BLESSINGS & GRATITUDE

•

•

•

PRAY: REQUESTS & RESULTS FOR YOURSELF & OTHERS

MEMORIZE: VERSE 4

Without reading or looking at the verse, try to say it from memory. After your attempt, look at the verse and see how close you were. Try to repeat the verse five more times, both out loud and silently, looking at the verse as needed.

TODAY . . . / . . . / . . . , I READ . . . .

WRITE: YOUR THOUGHTS & REFLECTIONS

FOCUS: ON YOUR PROGRESS AND GOALS

What is one mini action you can take in the next 24 hours that will move you a bit closer to your goal?

THANKS: BLESSINGS & GRATITUDE

- ...
- ...
- ...

PRAY: REQUESTS & RESULTS FOR YOURSELF & OTHERS

MEMORIZE: VERSE 4

Without reading or looking at the verse, try to write it from memory. After your attempt, look at the verse and see how close you were. Try to write the verse five times, and refer back to the verse after each attempt to see how well you did.

TODAY . . . / . . . / . . . , I READ . . . .

WRITE: YOUR THOUGHTS & REFLECTIONS

FOCUS: ON YOUR PROGRESS AND GOALS

Reread what you wrote for your Area of Focus and Support Pillars. Are you on the right track to hit your goals? Reaffirm your commitment to stay focused on improving this area of your life.

HANKS: BLESSINGS & GRATITUDE

RAY: REQUESTS & RESULTS FOR YOURSELF & OTHERS

MEMORIZE: VERSE 4

Say the verse and then write the verse from memory. Then, practice memorizing the verse using whichever technique you've liked the most—do it five times.

TODAY . . . / . . . / . . . , I READ . . . .

WRITE: YOUR THOUGHTS & REFLECTIONS

FOCUS: ON YOUR PROGRESS AND GOALS

Did you complete the action and mini action you set for yourself over the last 8 days? If so, how did it feel to make some progress? If not, what barriers prevented you from completing the actions you set for yourself?.

THANKS: BLESSINGS & GRATITUDE

- ....
- ....
- ....

PRAY: REQUESTS & RESULTS FOR YOURSELF & OTHERS

MEMORIZE: VERSE 4

Say the verse from memory. Pray the verse to God and ask him to help you apply what you have memorized and use it in your life. Write down an example of how knowing this verse from memory could be useful to you.

TODAY . . . / . . . / . . . , I READ . . . .

WRITE: YOUR THOUGHTS & REFLECTIONS

FOCUS: ON YOUR PROGRESS AND GOALS

What is one specific action you can take in the next week to move closer to your goal?

THANKS: BLESSINGS & GRATITUDE

-
-
-

PRAY: REQUESTS & RESULTS FOR YOURSELF & OTHERS

MEMORIZE: VERSE 5

Flip to page 14, and look at verse 5. Read the verse a few times and think about why this verse is important to you. Write down how having this verse memorized will help you in your walk with God.

TODAY ___/___/___, I READ ________________

WRITE: YOUR THOUGHTS & REFLECTIONS

FOCUS: ON YOUR PROGRESS AND GOALS

What challenge or temptation can you see yourself possibly having in the next couple of days related to your Area of Focus? How will you respond to this challenge if it arises?

HANKS: BLESSINGS & GRATITUDE

RAY: REQUESTS & RESULTS FOR YOURSELF & OTHERS

MEMORIZE: VERSE 5

Read the verse out loud five times and silently five times. Be sure to read the book name and verse number, as this is important to memorize also. Write the verse once.

TODAY ..../..../...., I READ ....

WRITE: YOUR THOUGHTS & REFLECTIONS

FOCUS: ON YOUR PROGRESS AND GOALS

Write a simple prayer to God, asking him to help you improve something specific related to your Area of Focus.

THANKS: BLESSINGS & GRATITUDE

-
-
-

PRAY: REQUESTS & RESULTS FOR YOURSELF & OTHERS

MEMORIZE: VERSE 5

Read the verse five times out loud. Write the verse five times. There are blank pages in the back of this journal that you can use.

TODAY ..../..../...., I READ ....

WRITE: YOUR THOUGHTS & REFLECTIONS

FOCUS: ON YOUR PROGRESS AND GOALS

Look up a bible verse that relates to your area of focus and write it below. Consider if this brings any new insight into your area of focus.

THANKS: BLESSINGS & GRATITUDE

-
-
-

PRAY: REQUESTS & RESULTS FOR YOURSELF & OTHERS

MEMORIZE: VERSE 5

Read the verse out loud once. Then write the verse five times and say the verse to yourself while you are writing.

TODAY ...../...../....., I READ ....

WRITE: YOUR THOUGHTS & REFLECTIONS

FOCUS: ON YOUR PROGRESS AND GOALS

Reflect on the positive progress you've made over the last few days, and write any thoughts about the success you've had so far.

HANKS: BLESSINGS & GRATITUDE

RAY: REQUESTS & RESULTS FOR YOURSELF & OTHERS

MEMORIZE: VERSE 5

Read the verse out loud once. Write the verse once. Now, without looking try to say the verse. Note where you have trouble and try to say the verse from memory five more times. Review the verse between each attempt to ensure you are correct.

TODAY ..../..../...., I READ ....

WRITE: YOUR THOUGHTS & REFLECTIONS

FOCUS: ON YOUR PROGRESS AND GOALS

Reflect on any difficulties you've had over the last few days, and write any thoughts about what was difficult.

THANKS: BLESSINGS & GRATITUDE

-
-
-

PRAY: REQUESTS & RESULTS FOR YOURSELF & OTHERS

MEMORIZE: VERSE 5

Without reading or looking at the verse, try to say it from memory. After your attempt, look at the verse and see how close you were. Try to repeat the verse five more times, both out loud and silently, looking at the verse as needed.

TODAY ..../..../...., I READ ....

WRITE: YOUR THOUGHTS & REFLECTIONS

FOCUS: ON YOUR PROGRESS AND GOALS

What is one mini action you can take in the next 24 hours that will move you a bit closer to your goal?

THANKS: BLESSINGS & GRATITUDE

- . . . .
- . . . .
- . . . .

PRAY: REQUESTS & RESULTS FOR YOURSELF & OTHERS

MEMORIZE: VERSE 5

Without reading or looking at the verse, try to write it from memory. After your attempt, look at the verse and see how close you were. Try to write the verse five times, and refer back to the verse after each attempt to see how well you did.

TODAY ... / ... / ... , I READ ...

WRITE: YOUR THOUGHTS & REFLECTIONS

FOCUS: ON YOUR PROGRESS AND GOALS

Reread what you wrote for your Area of Focus and Support Pillars. Are you on the right track to hit your goals? Reaffirm your commitment to stay focused on improving this area of your life.

HANKS: BLESSINGS & GRATITUDE

RAY: REQUESTS & RESULTS FOR YOURSELF & OTHERS

MEMORIZE: VERSE 5

Say the verse and then write the verse from memory. Then, practice memorizing the verse using whichever technique you've liked the most—do it five times.

TODAY . . . / . . . / . . . , I READ . . . .

WRITE: YOUR THOUGHTS & REFLECTIONS

FOCUS: ON YOUR PROGRESS AND GOALS

Did you complete the action and mini action you set for yourself over the last 8 days? If so, how did it feel to make some progress? If not, what barriers prevented you from completing the actions you set for yourself?.

THANKS: BLESSINGS & GRATITUDE

- ....
- ....
- ....

PRAY: REQUESTS & RESULTS FOR YOURSELF & OTHERS

MEMORIZE: VERSE 5

Say the verse from memory. Pray the verse to God and ask him to help you apply what you have memorized and use it in your life. Write down an example of how knowing this verse from memory could be useful to you.

TODAY . . . / . . . / . . . , I READ . . . .

WRITE: YOUR THOUGHTS & REFLECTIONS

FOCUS: ON YOUR PROGRESS AND GOALS

What is one specific action you can take in the next week to move closer to your goal?

THANKS: BLESSINGS & GRATITUDE

-
-
-

PRAY: REQUESTS & RESULTS FOR YOURSELF & OTHERS

MEMORIZE: VERSE 6

Flip to page 14, and look at verse 6. Read the verse a few times and think about why this verse is important to you. Write down how having this verse memorized will help you in your walk with God.

TODAY ..../..../...., I READ ....

WRITE: YOUR THOUGHTS & REFLECTIONS

FOCUS: ON YOUR PROGRESS AND GOALS

What challenge or temptation can you see yourself possibly having in the next couple of days related to your Area of Focus? How will you respond to this challenge if it arises?

HANKS: BLESSINGS & GRATITUDE

RAY: REQUESTS & RESULTS FOR YOURSELF & OTHERS

MEMORIZE: VERSE 6

Read the verse out loud five times and silently five times. Be sure to read the book name and verse number, as this is important to memorize also. Write the verse once.

TODAY ..../..../...., I READ ....

WRITE: YOUR THOUGHTS & REFLECTIONS

FOCUS: ON YOUR PROGRESS AND GOALS

Write a simple prayer to God, asking him to help you improve something specific related to your Area of Focus.

THANKS: BLESSINGS & GRATITUDE

- . . . .
- . . . .
- . . . .

PRAY: REQUESTS & RESULTS FOR YOURSELF & OTHERS

MEMORIZE: VERSE 6

Read the verse five times out loud. Write the verse five times. There are blank pages in the back of this journal that you can use.

TODAY . . . / . . . / . . . , I READ . . . .

WRITE: YOUR THOUGHTS & REFLECTIONS

FOCUS: ON YOUR PROGRESS AND GOALS

Look up a bible verse that relates to your area of focus and write it below. Consider if this brings any new insight into your area of focus.

THANKS: BLESSINGS & GRATITUDE

-
-
-

PRAY: REQUESTS & RESULTS FOR YOURSELF & OTHERS

MEMORIZE: VERSE 6

Read the verse out loud once. Then write the verse five times and say the verse to yourself while you are writing.

TODAY ...../...../....., I READ ....

WRITE: YOUR THOUGHTS & REFLECTIONS

FOCUS: ON YOUR PROGRESS AND GOALS

Reflect on the positive progress you've made over the last few days, and write any thoughts about the success you've had so far.

HANKS: BLESSINGS & GRATITUDE

RAY: REQUESTS & RESULTS FOR YOURSELF & OTHERS

MEMORIZE: VERSE 6

Read the verse out loud once. Write the verse once. Now, without looking try to say the verse. Note where you have trouble and try to say the verse from memory five more times. Review the verse between each attempt to ensure you are correct.

TODAY ..../..../...., I READ ....

WRITE: YOUR THOUGHTS & REFLECTIONS

FOCUS: ON YOUR PROGRESS AND GOALS

Reflect on any difficulties you've had over the last few days, and write any thoughts about what was difficult.

THANKS: BLESSINGS & GRATITUDE

- . . . .
- . . . .
- . . . .

PRAY: REQUESTS & RESULTS FOR YOURSELF & OTHERS

MEMORIZE: VERSE 6

Without reading or looking at the verse, try to say it from memory. After your attempt, look at the verse and see how close you were. Try to repeat the verse five more times, both out loud and silently, looking at the verse as needed.

TODAY . . . / . . . / . . . , I READ . . . .

WRITE: YOUR THOUGHTS & REFLECTIONS

FOCUS: ON YOUR PROGRESS AND GOALS

What is one mini action you can take in the next 24 hours that will move you a bit closer to your goal?

THANKS: BLESSINGS & GRATITUDE

-
-
-

PRAY: REQUESTS & RESULTS FOR YOURSELF & OTHERS

MEMORIZE: VERSE 6

Without reading or looking at the verse, try to write it from memory. After your attempt, look at the verse and see how close you were. Try to write the verse five times, and refer back to the verse after each attempt to see how well you did.

TODAY ..../..../...., I READ ....

WRITE: YOUR THOUGHTS & REFLECTIONS

FOCUS: ON YOUR PROGRESS AND GOALS

Reread what you wrote for your Area of Focus and Support Pillars. Are you on the right track to hit your goals? Reaffirm your commitment to stay focused on improving this area of your life.

HANKS: BLESSINGS & GRATITUDE

PRAY: REQUESTS & RESULTS FOR YOURSELF & OTHERS

MEMORIZE: VERSE 6

Say the verse and then write the verse from memory. Then, practice memorizing the verse using whichever technique you've liked the most—do it five times.

TODAY ..../..../...., I READ ....

WRITE: YOUR THOUGHTS & REFLECTIONS

FOCUS: ON YOUR PROGRESS AND GOALS

Did you complete the action and mini action you set for yourself over the last 8 days? If so, how did it feel to make some progress? If not, what barriers prevented you from completing the actions you set for yourself?.

THANKS: BLESSINGS & GRATITUDE

•

•

•

PRAY: REQUESTS & RESULTS FOR YOURSELF & OTHERS

MEMORIZE: VERSE 6

Say the verse from memory. Pray the verse to God and ask him to help you apply what you have memorized and use it in your life. Write down an example of how knowing this verse from memory could be useful to you.

TODAY . . . / . . . / . . . , I READ . . . .

WRITE: YOUR THOUGHTS & REFLECTIONS

FOCUS: ON YOUR PROGRESS AND GOALS

What is one specific action you can take in the next week to move closer to your goal?

THANKS: BLESSINGS & GRATITUDE

- . . . .
- . . . .
- . . . .

PRAY: REQUESTS & RESULTS FOR YOURSELF & OTHERS

MEMORIZE: VERSE 7

Flip to page 14, and look at verse 7. Read the verse a few times and think about why this verse is important to you. Write down how having this verse memorized will help you in your walk with God.

TODAY . . . / . . . / . . . , I READ . . . .

WRITE: YOUR THOUGHTS & REFLECTIONS

FOCUS: ON YOUR PROGRESS AND GOALS

What challenge or temptation can you see yourself possibly having in the next couple of days related to your Area of Focus? How will you respond to this challenge if it arises?

HANKS: BLESSINGS & GRATITUDE

PRAY: REQUESTS & RESULTS FOR YOURSELF & OTHERS

MEMORIZE: VERSE 7

Read the verse out loud five times and silently five times. Be sure to read the book name and verse number, as this is important to memorize also. Write the verse once.

TODAY ..../..../...., I READ ....

WRITE: YOUR THOUGHTS & REFLECTIONS

FOCUS: ON YOUR PROGRESS AND GOALS

Write a simple prayer to God, asking him to help you improve something specific related to your Area of Focus.

THANKS: BLESSINGS & GRATITUDE

-
-
-

PRAY: REQUESTS & RESULTS FOR YOURSELF & OTHERS

MEMORIZE: VERSE 7

Read the verse five times out loud. Write the verse five times. There are blank pages in the back of this journal that you can use.

TODAY ..../..../...., I READ ....

WRITE: YOUR THOUGHTS & REFLECTIONS

FOCUS: ON YOUR PROGRESS AND GOALS

Look up a bible verse that relates to your area of focus and write it below. Consider if this brings any new insight into your area of focus.

THANKS: BLESSINGS & GRATITUDE

-
-
-

PRAY: REQUESTS & RESULTS FOR YOURSELF & OTHERS

MEMORIZE: VERSE 7

Read the verse out loud once. Then write the verse five times and say the verse to yourself while you are writing.

TODAY ..../..../...., I READ ....

WRITE: YOUR THOUGHTS & REFLECTIONS

FOCUS: ON YOUR PROGRESS AND GOALS

Reflect on the positive progress you've made over the last few days, and write any thoughts about the success you've had so far.

HANKS: BLESSINGS & GRATITUDE

PRAY: REQUESTS & RESULTS FOR YOURSELF & OTHERS

MEMORIZE: VERSE 7

Read the verse out loud once. Write the verse once. Now, without looking try to say the verse. Note where you have trouble and try to say the verse from memory five more times. Review the verse between each attempt to ensure you are correct.

TODAY ..../..../...., I READ ....

WRITE: YOUR THOUGHTS & REFLECTIONS

FOCUS: ON YOUR PROGRESS AND GOALS

Reflect on any difficulties you've had over the last few days, and write any thoughts about what was difficult.

THANKS: BLESSINGS & GRATITUDE

-
-
-

PRAY: REQUESTS & RESULTS FOR YOURSELF & OTHERS

MEMORIZE: VERSE 7

Without reading or looking at the verse, try to say it from memory. After your attempt, look at the verse and see how close you were. Try to repeat the verse five more times, both out loud and silently, looking at the verse as needed.

TODAY ..../..../...., I READ ....

WRITE: YOUR THOUGHTS & REFLECTIONS

FOCUS: ON YOUR PROGRESS AND GOALS

What is one mini action you can take in the next 24 hours that will move you a bit closer to your goal?

THANKS: BLESSINGS & GRATITUDE

-
-
-

PRAY: REQUESTS & RESULTS FOR YOURSELF & OTHERS

MEMORIZE: VERSE 7

Without reading or looking at the verse, try to write it from memory. After your attempt, look at the verse and see how close you were. Try to write the verse five times, and refer back to the verse after each attempt to see how well you did.

TODAY . . . / . . . / . . . , I READ . . . .

WRITE: YOUR THOUGHTS & REFLECTIONS

FOCUS: ON YOUR PROGRESS AND GOALS

Reread what you wrote for your Area of Focus and Support Pillars. Are you on the right track to hit your goals? Reaffirm your commitment to stay focused on improving this area of your life.

THANKS: BLESSINGS & GRATITUDE

PRAY: REQUESTS & RESULTS FOR YOURSELF & OTHERS

MEMORIZE: VERSE 7

Say the verse and then write the verse from memory. Then, practice memorizing the verse using whichever technique you've liked the most—do it five times.

TODAY ..../..../...., I READ ....

WRITE: YOUR THOUGHTS & REFLECTIONS

FOCUS: ON YOUR PROGRESS AND GOALS

Did you complete the action and mini action you set for yourself over the last 8 days? If so, how did it feel to make some progress? If not, what barriers prevented you from completing the actions you set for yourself?.

THANKS: BLESSINGS & GRATITUDE

-
-
-

PRAY: REQUESTS & RESULTS FOR YOURSELF & OTHERS

MEMORIZE: VERSE 7

Say the verse from memory. Pray the verse to God and ask him to help you apply what you have memorized and use it in your life. Write down an example of how knowing this verse from memory could be useful to you.

TODAY . . . / . . . / . . . , I READ . . . .

WRITE: YOUR THOUGHTS & REFLECTIONS

FOCUS: ON YOUR PROGRESS AND GOALS

What is one specific action you can take in the next week to move closer to your goal?

THANKS: BLESSINGS & GRATITUDE

-
-
-

PRAY: REQUESTS & RESULTS FOR YOURSELF & OTHERS

MEMORIZE: VERSE 8

Flip to page 14, and look at verse 8. Read the verse a few times and think about why this verse is important to you. Write down how having this verse memorized will help you in your walk with God.

TODAY ..../..../...., I READ ....

WRITE: YOUR THOUGHTS & REFLECTIONS

FOCUS: ON YOUR PROGRESS AND GOALS

What challenge or temptation can you see yourself possibly having in the next couple of days related to your Area of Focus? How will you respond to this challenge if it arises?

HANKS: BLESSINGS & GRATITUDE

RAY: REQUESTS & RESULTS FOR YOURSELF & OTHERS

MEMORIZE: VERSE 8

Read the verse out loud five times and silently five times. Be sure to read the book name and verse number, as this is important to memorize also. Write the verse once.

TODAY ..../..../...., I READ ....

WRITE: YOUR THOUGHTS & REFLECTIONS

FOCUS: ON YOUR PROGRESS AND GOALS

Write a simple prayer to God, asking him to help you improve something specific related to your Area of Focus.

THANKS: BLESSINGS & GRATITUDE

-
-
-

PRAY: REQUESTS & RESULTS FOR YOURSELF & OTHERS

MEMORIZE: VERSE 8

Read the verse five times out loud. Write the verse five times. There are blank pages in the back of this journal that you can use.

TODAY . . . / . . . / . . . . , I READ . . . .

WRITE: YOUR THOUGHTS & REFLECTIONS

FOCUS: ON YOUR PROGRESS AND GOALS

Look up a bible verse that relates to your area of focus and write it below. Consider if this brings any new insight into your area of focus.

THANKS: BLESSINGS & GRATITUDE

- ....
- ....
- ....

PRAY: REQUESTS & RESULTS FOR YOURSELF & OTHERS

MEMORIZE: VERSE 8

Read the verse out loud once. Then write the verse five times and say the verse to yourself while you are writing.

TODAY ..../..../...., I READ ....

WRITE: YOUR THOUGHTS & REFLECTIONS

....

....

....

....

....

....

....

....

....

....

....

....

....

....

....

....

FOCUS: ON YOUR PROGRESS AND GOALS

Reflect on the positive progress you've made over the last few days, and write any thoughts about the success you've had so far.

....

....

....

....

HANKS: BLESSINGS & GRATITUDE

RAY: REQUESTS & RESULTS FOR YOURSELF & OTHERS

MEMORIZE: VERSE 8

Read the verse out loud once. Write the verse once. Now, without looking try to say the verse. Note where you have trouble and try to say the verse from memory five more times. Review the verse between each attempt to ensure you are correct.

TODAY ..../..../...., I READ ....

WRITE: YOUR THOUGHTS & REFLECTIONS

FOCUS: ON YOUR PROGRESS AND GOALS

Reflect on any difficulties you've had over the last few days, and write any thoughts about what was difficult.

THANKS: BLESSINGS & GRATITUDE

-
-
-

PRAY: REQUESTS & RESULTS FOR YOURSELF & OTHERS

MEMORIZE: VERSE 8

Without reading or looking at the verse, try to say it from memory. After your attempt, look at the verse and see how close you were. Try to repeat the verse five more times, both out loud and silently, looking at the verse as needed.

TODAY . . . / . . . / . . . , I READ . . . .

WRITE: YOUR THOUGHTS & REFLECTIONS

FOCUS: ON YOUR PROGRESS AND GOALS

What is one mini action you can take in the next 24 hours that will move you a bit closer to your goal?

THANKS: BLESSINGS & GRATITUDE

-
-
-

PRAY: REQUESTS & RESULTS FOR YOURSELF & OTHERS

MEMORIZE: VERSE 8

Without reading or looking at the verse, try to write it from memory. After your attempt, look at the verse and see how close you were. Try to write the verse five times, and refer back to the verse after each attempt to see how well you did.

TODAY ..../..../...., I READ ....

WRITE: YOUR THOUGHTS & REFLECTIONS

FOCUS: ON YOUR PROGRESS AND GOALS

Reread what you wrote for your Area of Focus and Support Pillars. Are you on the right track to hit your goals? Reaffirm your commitment to stay focused on improving this area of your life.

HANKS: BLESSINGS & GRATITUDE

RAY: REQUESTS & RESULTS FOR YOURSELF & OTHERS

MEMORIZE: VERSE 8

Say the verse and then write the verse from memory. Then, practice memorizing the verse using whichever technique you've liked the most—do it five times.

TODAY . . . / . . . / . . . , I READ . . . .

WRITE: YOUR THOUGHTS & REFLECTIONS

FOCUS: ON YOUR PROGRESS AND GOALS

Did you complete the action and mini action you set for yourself over the last 8 days? If so, how did it feel to make some progress? If not, what barriers prevented you from completing the actions you set for yourself?.

THANKS: BLESSINGS & GRATITUDE

- ....
- ....
- ....

PRAY: REQUESTS & RESULTS FOR YOURSELF & OTHERS

MEMORIZE: VERSE 8

Say the verse from memory. Pray the verse to God and ask him to help you apply what you have memorized and use it in your life. Write down an example of how knowing this verse from memory could be useful to you.

TODAY ..... / ..... / ..... , I READ ....

WRITE: YOUR THOUGHTS & REFLECTIONS

FOCUS: ON YOUR PROGRESS AND GOALS

What is one specific action you can take in the next week to move closer to your goal?

THANKS: BLESSINGS & GRATITUDE

-
-
-

PRAY: REQUESTS & RESULTS FOR YOURSELF & OTHERS

MEMORIZE: VERSE 9

Flip to page 14, and look at verse 9. Read the verse a few times and think about why this verse is important to you. Write down how having this verse memorized will help you in your walk with God.

TODAY ... / ... / ... , I READ ...

WRITE: YOUR THOUGHTS & REFLECTIONS

FOCUS: ON YOUR PROGRESS AND GOALS

What challenge or temptation can you see yourself possibly having in the next couple of days related to your Area of Focus? How will you respond to this challenge if it arises?

HANKS: BLESSINGS & GRATITUDE

RAY: REQUESTS & RESULTS FOR YOURSELF & OTHERS

MEMORIZE: VERSE 9

Read the verse out loud five times and silently five times. Be sure to read the book name and verse number, as this is important to memorize also. Write the verse once.

TODAY . . . / . . . / . . . , I READ . . . .

WRITE: YOUR THOUGHTS & REFLECTIONS

FOCUS: ON YOUR PROGRESS AND GOALS

Write a simple prayer to God, asking him to help you improve something specific related to your Area of Focus.

THANKS: BLESSINGS & GRATITUDE

-
-
-

PRAY: REQUESTS & RESULTS FOR YOURSELF & OTHERS

MEMORIZE: VERSE 9

Read the verse five times out loud. Write the verse five times. There are blank pages in the back of this journal that you can use.

TODAY ..../..../...., I READ ....

WRITE: YOUR THOUGHTS & REFLECTIONS

FOCUS: ON YOUR PROGRESS AND GOALS

Look up a bible verse that relates to your area of focus and write it below. Consider if this brings any new insight into your area of focus.

THANKS: BLESSINGS & GRATITUDE

-
-
-

PRAY: REQUESTS & RESULTS FOR YOURSELF & OTHERS

MEMORIZE: VERSE 9

Read the verse out loud once. Then write the verse five times and say the verse to yourself while you are writing.

TODAY ..../..../...., I READ ....

WRITE: YOUR THOUGHTS & REFLECTIONS

FOCUS: ON YOUR PROGRESS AND GOALS

Reflect on the positive progress you've made over the last few days, and write any thoughts about the success you've had so far.

HANKS: BLESSINGS & GRATITUDE

RAY: REQUESTS & RESULTS FOR YOURSELF & OTHERS

MEMORIZE: VERSE 9

Read the verse out loud once. Write the verse once. Now, without looking try to say the verse. Note where you have trouble and try to say the verse from memory five more times. Review the verse between each attempt to ensure you are correct.

TODAY . . . / . . . / . . . , I READ . . . .

WRITE: YOUR THOUGHTS & REFLECTIONS

FOCUS: ON YOUR PROGRESS AND GOALS

Reflect on any difficulties you've had over the last few days, and write any thoughts about what was difficult.

THANKS: BLESSINGS & GRATITUDE

PRAY: REQUESTS & RESULTS FOR YOURSELF & OTHERS

MEMORIZE: VERSE 9

Without reading or looking at the verse, try to say it from memory. After your attempt, look at the verse and see how close you were. Try to repeat the verse five more times, both out loud and silently, looking at the verse as needed.

TODAY . . . / . . . / . . . , I READ . . . .

WRITE: YOUR THOUGHTS & REFLECTIONS

FOCUS: ON YOUR PROGRESS AND GOALS

What is one mini action you can take in the next 24 hours that will move you a bit closer to your goal?

THANKS: BLESSINGS & GRATITUDE

- ....
- ....
- ....

PRAY: REQUESTS & RESULTS FOR YOURSELF & OTHERS

....

....

....

....

....

....

....

....

....

....

....

....

....

MEMORIZE: VERSE 9

Without reading or looking at the verse, try to write it from memory. After your attempt, look at the verse and see how close you were. Try to write the verse five times, and refer back to the verse after each attempt to see how well you did.

....

....

....

....

TODAY ...../...../....., I READ ....

WRITE: YOUR THOUGHTS & REFLECTIONS

FOCUS: ON YOUR PROGRESS AND GOALS

Reread what you wrote for your Area of Focus and Support Pillars. Are you on the right track to hit your goals? Reaffirm your commitment to stay focused on improving this area of your life.

HANKS: BLESSINGS & GRATITUDE

RAY: REQUESTS & RESULTS FOR YOURSELF & OTHERS

MEMORIZE: VERSE 9

Say the verse and then write the verse from memory. Then, practice memorizing the verse using whichever technique you've liked the most—do it five times.

TODAY . . . / . . . / . . . , I READ . . . .

WRITE: YOUR THOUGHTS & REFLECTIONS

FOCUS: ON YOUR PROGRESS AND GOALS

Did you complete the action and mini action you set for yourself over the last 8 days? If so, how did it feel to make some progress? If not, what barriers prevented you from completing the actions you set for yourself?.

THANKS: BLESSINGS & GRATITUDE

-
-
-

PRAY: REQUESTS & RESULTS FOR YOURSELF & OTHERS

MEMORIZE: VERSE 9

Say the verse from memory. Pray the verse to God and ask him to help you apply what you have memorized and use it in your life. Write down an example of how knowing this verse from memory could be useful to you.

TODAY . . . / . . . / . . . , I READ . . . .

WRITE: YOUR THOUGHTS & REFLECTIONS

FOCUS: ON YOUR PROGRESS AND GOALS

Nine more days until the journey is over. Read your Area of Focus again at the beginning of the journal. What is one final specific action you can take in the next week to move closer to or complete your goal?

THANKS: BLESSINGS & GRATITUDE

-
-
-

PRAY: REQUESTS & RESULTS FOR YOURSELF & OTHERS

MEMORIZE: REVISIT VERSE 1

Can you say verse 1 from memory without looking at it? If so, congrats! If not, don't worry—just read the verse and try to say it again. Scripture memorization isn't a one time thing, it helps to reread the verse every once in a while to brush up.

TODAY ..../..../...., I READ ....

WRITE: YOUR THOUGHTS & REFLECTIONS

FOCUS: ON YOUR PROGRESS AND GOALS

What challenge or temptation can you see yourself possibly having in this final stretch? How will you respond to this challenge if it arises? Can you finish strong and make no excuses?

HANKS: BLESSINGS & GRATITUDE

RAY: REQUESTS & RESULTS FOR YOURSELF & OTHERS

MEMORIZE: REVISIT VERSE 2

Can you say verse 2 from memory without looking at it? If so, well done! If not, don't worry—just read the verse and try to say it again until you get it right. Consider saving or bookmarking your verses in a Bible app as a way to easily reread them all.

TODAY ..../..../...., I READ ....

WRITE: YOUR THOUGHTS & REFLECTIONS

FOCUS: ON YOUR PROGRESS AND GOALS

Write a simple prayer to God, asking him to help you finish strong and continue to improve in your Area of Focus even after the Near Journal is completed.

THANKS: BLESSINGS & GRATITUDE

-
-
-

PRAY: REQUESTS & RESULTS FOR YOURSELF & OTHERS

MEMORIZE: REVISIT VERSE 3

Can you say verse 3 from memory without looking at it? If so, awesome! If not, don't worry—just read the verse and try to say it again until you get it right. You can set calendar reminders in your phone at random intervals to remind you of your verses.

TODAY . . . / . . . / . . . , I READ . . . .

WRITE: YOUR THOUGHTS & REFLECTIONS

FOCUS: ON YOUR PROGRESS AND GOALS

Look up a bible verse that relates to your area of focus and write it below. Think about all the different new verses you've discovered over the past 90 days.

THANKS: BLESSINGS & GRATITUDE

-
-
-

PRAY: REQUESTS & RESULTS FOR YOURSELF & OTHERS

MEMORIZE: REVISIT VERSE 4

Can you say verse 4 from memory without looking at it? If so, nice! If not, don't worry—just read the verse and try to say it again until you get it right.

TODAY ..../..../...., I READ ....

WRITE: YOUR THOUGHTS & REFLECTIONS

FOCUS: ON YOUR PROGRESS AND GOALS

Reflect on the positive progress you've made over the last 90 days, and write any thoughts about the success you've had.

HANKS: BLESSINGS & GRATITUDE

RAY: REQUESTS & RESULTS FOR YOURSELF & OTHERS

MEMORIZE: REVISIT VERSE 5

Can you say verse 5 from memory without looking at it? If so, good job! If not, don't worry—just read the verse and try to say it again until you get it right. Write a verse you're having trouble with on a sticky note and put it somewhere you'll see it a lot.

TODAY ..../..../...., I READ ....

WRITE: YOUR THOUGHTS & REFLECTIONS

FOCUS: ON YOUR PROGRESS AND GOALS

Reflect on any difficulties you've had over the last 90 days, and write any thoughts about what was difficult.

THANKS: BLESSINGS & GRATITUDE

-
-
-

PRAY: REQUESTS & RESULTS FOR YOURSELF & OTHERS

MEMORIZE: REVISIT VERSE 6

Can you say verse 6 from memory without looking at it? If so, well done! If not, don't worry—just read the verse and try to say it again until you get it right. Repetition is the key to memorization, so be sure to keep looking at and saying your verses.

TODAY ..../..../...., I READ ....

WRITE: YOUR THOUGHTS & REFLECTIONS

FOCUS: ON YOUR PROGRESS AND GOALS

What is one final mini action you can take in the next 24 hours that will give you a feeling of satisfaction as you wrap up your goal?

THANKS: BLESSINGS & GRATITUDE

-
-
-

PRAY: REQUESTS & RESULTS FOR YOURSELF & OTHERS

MEMORIZE: REVISIT VERSE 7

Can you say verse 7 from memory without looking at it? If so, congrats! If not, don't worry—just read the verse and try to say it again until you get it right. Sometimes, even knowing a couple words from a verse can help you through a rough situation.

TODAY . . . / . . . / . . . , I READ . . . .

WRITE: YOUR THOUGHTS & REFLECTIONS

FOCUS: ON YOUR PROGRESS AND GOALS

Reread what you wrote for your Area of Focus and Support Pillars. Did you improve your Area of Focus and make progress on your Support Pillars? Are there any final things you need to wrap up to be satisfied?

HANKS: BLESSINGS & GRATITUDE

RAY: REQUESTS & RESULTS FOR YOURSELF & OTHERS

MEMORIZE: REVISIT VERSE 8

Can you say verse 8 from memory without looking at it? If so, well done! If not, don't worry—just read the verse and try to say it again until you get it right.

TODAY ___/___/___, I READ ______________________

WRITE: YOUR THOUGHTS & REFLECTIONS

FOCUS: ON YOUR PROGRESS AND GOALS

Spend some time praying and reflecting on the things you've done and the progress you've made over the last 90 days. Lasting change happens one step at a time, and you are on the right path. Thank God for helping you improve in your Area of Focus.

THANKS: BLESSINGS & GRATITUDE

-
-
-

PRAY: REQUESTS & RESULTS FOR YOURSELF & OTHERS

MEMORIZE: REVISIT VERSE 9

Can you say verse 9 from memory without looking at it? If so, well done! If not, don't worry—just read the verse and try to say it again until you get it right. You've made it. Nine verses. Way to go! Take a moment to thank God for helping you memorize.

We are deeply honored that you chose the Near Journal.

If you enjoyed the journal, or like what we have created, can I ask a personal favor? Please tell a friend about it. Your support enables us to help more people transform their relationship with God.

We are committed to giving free copies of the *Near Journal* away to new believers, so the more we sell, the more we can give.

Connect with us on social media **@drawnearco**. We are active on Instagram, Twitter, Facebook, and online at **www.drawnear.co**. Shoot us a picture of how YOU use the *Near Journal*.

Peace and Love,
Jacob

DRAW NEAR CO